Mileage Log

_____

_____

_____

Mileage Log

MAKE _____ MODEL _____ YEAR _____

DATE	BUSINESS PURPOSE	ODOMETER		TOTAL MILES
		BEGIN	END	
TOTAL				

Mileage Log

MAKE _____ MODEL _____ YEAR _____

| DATE | BUSINESS PURPOSE | ODOMETER | | TOTAL MILES |
		BEGIN	END	
TOTAL				

Mileage Log

MAKE _____ MODEL _____ YEAR _____

| DATE | BUSINESS PURPOSE | ODOMETER | | TOTAL MILES |
		BEGIN	END	
TOTAL				

Mileage Log

MAKE _____ MODEL _____ YEAR _____

DATE	BUSINESS PURPOSE	ODOMETER		TOTAL MILES
		BEGIN	END	
TOTAL				

Mileage Log

MAKE _____ MODEL _____ YEAR _____

DATE	BUSINESS PURPOSE	ODOMETER		TOTAL MILES
		BEGIN	END	
TOTAL				

Mileage Log

MAKE _____ MODEL _____ YEAR _____

| DATE | BUSINESS PURPOSE | ODOMETER | | TOTAL MILES |
		BEGIN	END	
TOTAL				

Mileage Log

MAKE _____ MODEL _____ YEAR _____

| DATE | BUSINESS PURPOSE | ODOMETER | | TOTAL MILES |
		BEGIN	END	
TOTAL				

Mileage Log

MAKE _____ MODEL _____ YEAR _____

| DATE | BUSINESS PURPOSE | ODOMETER | | TOTAL MILES |
		BEGIN	END	
TOTAL				

Mileage Log

MAKE _____ MODEL _____ YEAR _____

DATE	BUSINESS PURPOSE	ODOMETER		TOTAL MILES
		BEGIN	END	
TOTAL				

Mileage Log

MAKE _____ MODEL _____ YEAR _____

DATE	BUSINESS PURPOSE	ODOMETER		TOTAL MILES
		BEGIN	END	
TOTAL				

Mileage Log

MAKE _____ MODEL _____ YEAR _____

| DATE | BUSINESS PURPOSE | ODOMETER | | TOTAL MILES |
		BEGIN	END	
TOTAL				

Mileage Log

MAKE _____ MODEL _____ YEAR _____

| DATE | BUSINESS PURPOSE | ODOMETER | | TOTAL MILES |
		BEGIN	END	
TOTAL				

Mileage Log

MAKE _____ MODEL _____ YEAR _____

| DATE | BUSINESS PURPOSE | ODOMETER | | TOTAL MILES |
		BEGIN	END	
TOTAL				

Mileage Log

MAKE _____ MODEL _____ YEAR _____

| DATE | BUSINESS PURPOSE | ODOMETER | | TOTAL MILES |
		BEGIN	END	
TOTAL				

Mileage Log

MAKE _____ MODEL _____ YEAR _____

DATE	BUSINESS PURPOSE	ODOMETER		TOTAL MILES
		BEGIN	END	
TOTAL				

Mileage Log

MAKE _____ MODEL _____ YEAR _____

DATE	BUSINESS PURPOSE	ODOMETER		TOTAL MILES
		BEGIN	END	
TOTAL				

Mileage Log

MAKE _____ MODEL _____ YEAR _____

DATE	BUSINESS PURPOSE	ODOMETER		TOTAL MILES
		BEGIN	END	
TOTAL				

Mileage Log

MAKE _____ MODEL _____ YEAR _____

| DATE | BUSINESS PURPOSE | ODOMETER | | TOTAL MILES |
		BEGIN	END	
TOTAL				

Mileage Log

MAKE _____ MODEL _____ YEAR _____

| DATE | BUSINESS PURPOSE | ODOMETER | | TOTAL MILES |
		BEGIN	END	
TOTAL				

Mileage Log

MAKE _____ MODEL _____ YEAR _____

| DATE | BUSINESS PURPOSE | ODOMETER | | TOTAL MILES |
		BEGIN	END	
TOTAL				

Mileage Log

MAKE _____ MODEL _____ YEAR _____

| DATE | BUSINESS PURPOSE | ODOMETER | | TOTAL MILES |
		BEGIN	END	
TOTAL				

Mileage Log

MAKE _____ MODEL _____ YEAR _____

| DATE | BUSINESS PURPOSE | ODOMETER | | TOTAL MILES |
		BEGIN	END	
TOTAL				

Mileage Log

MAKE _____ MODEL _____ YEAR _____

| DATE | BUSINESS PURPOSE | ODOMETER | | TOTAL MILES |
		BEGIN	END	
TOTAL				

Mileage Log

MAKE _____ MODEL _____ YEAR _____

| DATE | BUSINESS PURPOSE | ODOMETER | | TOTAL MILES |
		BEGIN	END	
TOTAL				

Mileage Log

MAKE _____ MODEL _____ YEAR _____

| DATE | BUSINESS PURPOSE | ODOMETER | | TOTAL MILES |
		BEGIN	END	
TOTAL				

Mileage Log

MAKE _____ MODEL _____ YEAR _____

| DATE | BUSINESS PURPOSE | ODOMETER | | TOTAL MILES |
		BEGIN	END	
TOTAL				

Mileage Log

MAKE _____ MODEL _____ YEAR _____

| DATE | BUSINESS PURPOSE | ODOMETER | | TOTAL MILES |
		BEGIN	END	
TOTAL				

Mileage Log

MAKE _____ MODEL _____ YEAR _____

| DATE | BUSINESS PURPOSE | ODOMETER | | TOTAL MILES |
		BEGIN	END	
TOTAL				

Mileage **Log**

MAKE _____ MODEL _____ YEAR _____

DATE	BUSINESS PURPOSE	ODOMETER		TOTAL MILES
		BEGIN	END	
TOTAL				

Mileage Log

MAKE _____ MODEL _____ YEAR _____

| DATE | BUSINESS PURPOSE | ODOMETER | | TOTAL MILES |
		BEGIN	END	
TOTAL				

Mileage Log

MAKE _____ MODEL _____ YEAR _____

| DATE | BUSINESS PURPOSE | ODOMETER | | TOTAL MILES |
		BEGIN	END	
TOTAL				

Mileage Log

MAKE _____ MODEL _____ YEAR _____

| DATE | BUSINESS PURPOSE | ODOMETER | | TOTAL MILES |
		BEGIN	END	
TOTAL				

Mileage Log

MAKE _____ MODEL _____ YEAR _____

| DATE | BUSINESS PURPOSE | ODOMETER | | TOTAL MILES |
		BEGIN	END	
TOTAL				

Mileage Log

MAKE _____ MODEL _____ YEAR _____

| DATE | BUSINESS PURPOSE | ODOMETER | | TOTAL MILES |
		BEGIN	END	
TOTAL				

Mileage Log

MAKE _____ MODEL _____ YEAR _____

| DATE | BUSINESS PURPOSE | ODOMETER | | TOTAL MILES |
		BEGIN	END	
TOTAL				

Mileage Log

MAKE _____ MODEL _____ YEAR _____

| DATE | BUSINESS PURPOSE | ODOMETER | | TOTAL MILES |
		BEGIN	END	
TOTAL				

Mileage Log

MAKE _____ MODEL _____ YEAR _____

| DATE | BUSINESS PURPOSE | ODOMETER | | TOTAL MILES |
		BEGIN	END	
TOTAL				

Mileage Log

MAKE _____ MODEL _____ YEAR _____

| DATE | BUSINESS PURPOSE | ODOMETER | | TOTAL MILES |
		BEGIN	END	
TOTAL				

Mileage Log

MAKE _____ MODEL _____ YEAR _____

| DATE | BUSINESS PURPOSE | ODOMETER | | TOTAL MILES |
		BEGIN	END	
TOTAL				

Mileage Log

MAKE _____ MODEL _____ YEAR _____

DATE	BUSINESS PURPOSE	ODOMETER		TOTAL MILES
		BEGIN	END	
TOTAL				

Mileage Log

MAKE _____ MODEL _____ YEAR _____

| DATE | BUSINESS PURPOSE | ODOMETER | | TOTAL MILES |
		BEGIN	END	
TOTAL				

Mileage Log

MAKE _____ MODEL _____ YEAR _____

DATE	BUSINESS PURPOSE	ODOMETER		TOTAL MILES
		BEGIN	END	
TOTAL				

Mileage Log

MAKE _____ MODEL _____ YEAR _____

| DATE | BUSINESS PURPOSE | ODOMETER | | TOTAL MILES |
		BEGIN	END	
TOTAL				

Mileage Log

MAKE _____ MODEL _____ YEAR _____

| DATE | BUSINESS PURPOSE | ODOMETER | | TOTAL MILES |
		BEGIN	END	
TOTAL				

Mileage Log

MAKE _____ MODEL _____ YEAR _____

| DATE | BUSINESS PURPOSE | ODOMETER | | TOTAL MILES |
		BEGIN	END	
TOTAL				

Mileage Log

MAKE _____ MODEL _____ YEAR _____

DATE	BUSINESS PURPOSE	ODOMETER		TOTAL MILES
		BEGIN	END	
TOTAL				

Mileage Log

MAKE _____ MODEL _____ YEAR _____

| DATE | BUSINESS PURPOSE | ODOMETER | | TOTAL MILES |
		BEGIN	END	
TOTAL				

Mileage Log

MAKE _____ MODEL _____ YEAR _____

| DATE | BUSINESS PURPOSE | ODOMETER | | TOTAL MILES |
		BEGIN	END	
TOTAL				

Mileage Log

MAKE _____ MODEL _____ YEAR _____

| DATE | BUSINESS PURPOSE | ODOMETER | | TOTAL MILES |
		BEGIN	END	
TOTAL				

Mileage Log

MAKE _____ MODEL _____ YEAR _____

| DATE | BUSINESS PURPOSE | ODOMETER | | TOTAL MILES |
		BEGIN	END	
TOTAL				

Mileage Log

MAKE _____ MODEL _____ YEAR _____

DATE	BUSINESS PURPOSE	ODOMETER		TOTAL MILES
		BEGIN	END	
TOTAL				

Mileage Log

MAKE _____ MODEL _____ YEAR _____

| DATE | BUSINESS PURPOSE | ODOMETER | | TOTAL MILES |
		BEGIN	END	
TOTAL				

Mileage Log

MAKE _____ MODEL _____ YEAR _____

DATE	BUSINESS PURPOSE	ODOMETER		TOTAL MILES
		BEGIN	END	
TOTAL				

Mileage **Mileage** Log

MAKE _____ MODEL _____ YEAR _____

DATE	BUSINESS PURPOSE	ODOMETER		TOTAL MILES
		BEGIN	END	
TOTAL				

Mileage Log

MAKE _____ MODEL _____ YEAR _____

| DATE | BUSINESS PURPOSE | ODOMETER | | TOTAL MILES |
		BEGIN	END	
TOTAL				

Mileage Log

MAKE _____ MODEL _____ YEAR _____

| DATE | BUSINESS PURPOSE | ODOMETER | | TOTAL MILES |
		BEGIN	END	
TOTAL				

Mileage Log

MAKE _____ MODEL _____ YEAR _____

| DATE | BUSINESS PURPOSE | ODOMETER | | TOTAL MILES |
		BEGIN	END	
TOTAL				

Mileage Log

MAKE _____ MODEL _____ YEAR _____

| DATE | BUSINESS PURPOSE | ODOMETER | | TOTAL MILES |
		BEGIN	END	
TOTAL				

Mileage Log

MAKE _____ MODEL _____ YEAR _____

| DATE | BUSINESS PURPOSE | ODOMETER | | TOTAL MILES |
		BEGIN	END	
TOTAL				

Mileage Log

MAKE _____ MODEL _____ YEAR _____

| DATE | BUSINESS PURPOSE | ODOMETER | | TOTAL MILES |
		BEGIN	END	
TOTAL				

Mileage Log

MAKE _____ MODEL _____ YEAR _____

DATE	BUSINESS PURPOSE	ODOMETER		TOTAL MILES
		BEGIN	END	
TOTAL				

Mileage Log

MAKE _____ MODEL _____ YEAR _____

| DATE | BUSINESS PURPOSE | ODOMETER | | TOTAL MILES |
		BEGIN	END	
TOTAL				

Mileage Log

MAKE _____ MODEL _____ YEAR _____

| DATE | BUSINESS PURPOSE | ODOMETER | | TOTAL MILES |
		BEGIN	END	
TOTAL				

Mileage Log

MAKE _____ MODEL _____ YEAR _____

| DATE | BUSINESS PURPOSE | ODOMETER | | TOTAL MILES |
		BEGIN	END	
TOTAL				

Mileage Log

MAKE _____ MODEL _____ YEAR _____

| DATE | BUSINESS PURPOSE | ODOMETER | | TOTAL MILES |
		BEGIN	END	
TOTAL				

Mileage Log

MAKE _____ MODEL _____ YEAR _____

| DATE | BUSINESS PURPOSE | ODOMETER | | TOTAL MILES |
		BEGIN	END	
TOTAL				

Mileage Log

MAKE _____ MODEL _____ YEAR _____

| DATE | BUSINESS PURPOSE | ODOMETER | | TOTAL MILES |
		BEGIN	END	
TOTAL				

Mileage Log

MAKE _____ MODEL _____ YEAR _____

DATE	BUSINESS PURPOSE	ODOMETER		TOTAL MILES
		BEGIN	END	
TOTAL				

Mileage Log

MAKE _____ MODEL _____ YEAR _____

| DATE | BUSINESS PURPOSE | ODOMETER | | TOTAL MILES |
		BEGIN	END	
TOTAL				

Mileage Log

MAKE _____ MODEL _____ YEAR _____

| DATE | BUSINESS PURPOSE | ODOMETER | | TOTAL MILES |
		BEGIN	END	
TOTAL				

Mileage Log

MAKE _____ MODEL _____ YEAR _____

| DATE | BUSINESS PURPOSE | ODOMETER | | TOTAL MILES |
		BEGIN	END	
TOTAL				

Mileage Log

MAKE _____ MODEL _____ YEAR _____

| DATE | BUSINESS PURPOSE | ODOMETER | | TOTAL MILES |
		BEGIN	END	
TOTAL				

Mileage Log

MAKE _____ MODEL _____ YEAR _____

| DATE | BUSINESS PURPOSE | ODOMETER | | TOTAL MILES |
		BEGIN	END	
TOTAL				

Mileage Log

MAKE _____ MODEL _____ YEAR _____

| DATE | BUSINESS PURPOSE | ODOMETER | | TOTAL MILES |
		BEGIN	END	
TOTAL				

Mileage Log

MAKE _____ MODEL _____ YEAR _____

DATE	BUSINESS PURPOSE	ODOMETER		TOTAL MILES
		BEGIN	END	
TOTAL				

Mileage Log

MAKE _____ MODEL _____ YEAR _____

| DATE | BUSINESS PURPOSE | ODOMETER | | TOTAL MILES |
		BEGIN	END	
TOTAL				

Mileage Log

MAKE _____ MODEL _____ YEAR _____

| DATE | BUSINESS PURPOSE | ODOMETER | | TOTAL MILES |
		BEGIN	END	
TOTAL				

Mileage Log

MAKE _____ MODEL _____ YEAR _____

| DATE | BUSINESS PURPOSE | ODOMETER | | TOTAL MILES |
		BEGIN	END	
TOTAL				

Mileage Log

MAKE _____ MODEL _____ YEAR _____

| DATE | BUSINESS PURPOSE | ODOMETER | | TOTAL MILES |
		BEGIN	END	
TOTAL				

Mileage Log

MAKE _____ MODEL _____ YEAR _____

DATE	BUSINESS PURPOSE	ODOMETER		TOTAL MILES
		BEGIN	END	
TOTAL				

Mileage Log

MAKE _____ MODEL _____ YEAR _____

| DATE | BUSINESS PURPOSE | ODOMETER | | TOTAL MILES |
		BEGIN	END	
TOTAL				

Mileage Log

MAKE _____ MODEL _____ YEAR _____

| DATE | BUSINESS PURPOSE | ODOMETER | | TOTAL MILES |
		BEGIN	END	
TOTAL				

Mileage Log

MAKE _____ MODEL _____ YEAR _____

| DATE | BUSINESS PURPOSE | ODOMETER | | TOTAL MILES |
		BEGIN	END	
TOTAL				

Mileage Log

MAKE _____ MODEL _____ YEAR _____

| DATE | BUSINESS PURPOSE | ODOMETER | | TOTAL MILES |
		BEGIN	END	
TOTAL				

Mileage Log

MAKE _____ MODEL _____ YEAR _____

| DATE | BUSINESS PURPOSE | ODOMETER | | TOTAL MILES |
		BEGIN	END	
TOTAL				

Mileage Log

MAKE _____ MODEL _____ YEAR _____

| DATE | BUSINESS PURPOSE | ODOMETER | | TOTAL MILES |
		BEGIN	END	
TOTAL				

Mileage Log

MAKE _____ MODEL _____ YEAR _____

| DATE | BUSINESS PURPOSE | ODOMETER | | TOTAL MILES |
		BEGIN	END	
TOTAL				

Mileage Log

MAKE _____ MODEL _____ YEAR _____

DATE	BUSINESS PURPOSE	ODOMETER		TOTAL MILES
		BEGIN	END	
TOTAL				

Mileage Log

MAKE _____ MODEL _____ YEAR _____

| DATE | BUSINESS PURPOSE | ODOMETER | | TOTAL MILES |
		BEGIN	END	
TOTAL				

Mileage Log

MAKE _____ MODEL _____ YEAR _____

| DATE | BUSINESS PURPOSE | ODOMETER | | TOTAL MILES |
		BEGIN	END	
TOTAL				

Mileage Log

MAKE _____ MODEL _____ YEAR _____

DATE	BUSINESS PURPOSE	ODOMETER		TOTAL MILES
		BEGIN	END	
TOTAL				

Mileage Log

MAKE _____ MODEL _____ YEAR _____

| DATE | BUSINESS PURPOSE | ODOMETER | | TOTAL MILES |
		BEGIN	END	
TOTAL				

Mileage Log

MAKE _____ MODEL _____ YEAR _____

| DATE | BUSINESS PURPOSE | ODOMETER | | TOTAL MILES |
		BEGIN	END	
TOTAL				

Mileage Log

MAKE _____ MODEL _____ YEAR _____

| DATE | BUSINESS PURPOSE | ODOMETER | | TOTAL MILES |
		BEGIN	END	
TOTAL				

Mileage Log

MAKE _____ MODEL _____ YEAR _____

DATE	BUSINESS PURPOSE	ODOMETER		TOTAL MILES
		BEGIN	END	
TOTAL				

Mileage Log

MAKE _____ MODEL _____ YEAR _____

| DATE | BUSINESS PURPOSE | ODOMETER | | TOTAL MILES |
		BEGIN	END	
TOTAL				

Mileage Log

MAKE _____ MODEL _____ YEAR _____

| DATE | BUSINESS PURPOSE | ODOMETER | | TOTAL MILES |
		BEGIN	END	
TOTAL				

Mileage Log

MAKE _____ MODEL _____ YEAR _____

| DATE | BUSINESS PURPOSE | ODOMETER | | TOTAL MILES |
		BEGIN	END	
TOTAL				

Mileage Log

MAKE _____ MODEL _____ YEAR _____

| DATE | BUSINESS PURPOSE | ODOMETER | | TOTAL MILES |
		BEGIN	END	
TOTAL				

Mileage Log

MAKE _____ MODEL _____ YEAR _____

| DATE | BUSINESS PURPOSE | ODOMETER | | TOTAL MILES |
		BEGIN	END	
TOTAL				

Yearly Mileage

MAKE _____ MODEL _____ YEAR _____

TAX YEAR _____	
TOTAL MILES	
BUSINESS MILES	
PERSONAL MILES	

NOTES

_____

_____

_____

_____

_____

_____

_____

Yearly Mileage

MAKE _____ MODEL _____ YEAR _____

TAX YEAR _____

TOTAL MILES	
BUSINESS MILES	
PERSONAL MILES	

NOTES

Yearly Mileage

MAKE _____ MODEL _____ YEAR _____

TAX YEAR _____

TOTAL MILES	
BUSINESS MILES	
PERSONAL MILES	

NOTES

Yearly Mileage

MAKE _____   MODEL _____   YEAR _____

TAX YEAR _____

TOTAL MILES	
BUSINESS MILES	
PERSONAL MILES	

NOTES

Yearly Mileage

MAKE _____ MODEL _____ YEAR _____

TAX YEAR _____

TOTAL MILES	
BUSINESS MILES	
PERSONAL MILES	

NOTES

Yearly Mileage

MAKE _____ MODEL _____ YEAR _____

TAX YEAR _____

TOTAL MILES	
BUSINESS MILES	
PERSONAL MILES	

NOTES

Yearly Mileage

MAKE _____ MODEL _____ YEAR _____

TAX YEAR _____

TOTAL MILES	
BUSINESS MILES	
PERSONAL MILES	

NOTES

Made in the USA
Las Vegas, NV
17 February 2022

44094729R00066